Strange Conveyances

Poems By

M. V. Montgomery

Plain View Press
P.O. 42255
Austin, TX 78704

plainviewpress.net
sb@plainviewpress.net
512-441-2452

Copyright © 2010 M.V. Montgomery. All rights reserved under International and Pan-American Copyright Conventions. No part of this book may be reproduced or distributed in any form or by any means, or stored in a data base or retrieval system, without written permission from the author. All rights, including electronic, are reserved by the author and publisher.

ISBN: 978-1-935514-67-1
Library of Congress Number: 2010929927

Cover art "From Somewhere to Elsewhere" by Vivien Blackett.
Cover design by Susan Bright.

Contents

Pathways — 7

    Pathways — 9
    First Memory — 10
    Primal — 11
    The House At the Bottom Of the Lake — 13
    Men Of Thor — 14
    My Lost Years: The Sonnet — 16
    My Dream Of Mill Valley — 17
    To a Former Brother-In-Law — 19
    Three Failed Transactions — 20
    Five Reasons My Dream Of Tucson Was Impossible — 23
    Homecoming Flood — 25

Animal Myths — 27

    Animal Myths — 29
    A Flower — 30
    The Bear — 31
    The Earth Witch — 32
    Back There — 33
    Dog's Body — 34
    Stendhal's Mirror — 36
    Rainforest Honeymoon — 40
    The Truth About Lemmings — 41
    A Dictionary Of Animal Symbols — 42
    I Wish You Many Bats — 46

Ghosts   47

    Ghosts   49
    Dream After *Rashomon*   50
    Homunculus   51
    Eminent Domain   52
    Blood Sacrifice   53
    Frankenstein   54
    I Was Dead: 55
    My Little Murder   56
    Zombie Peace   57
    Satanic Lunch   58
    Letter To Buffy   61

A Tapestry of Saints   63

    Woman At the Kroger   65
    Katie O   66
    That Man   67
    A Tapestry Of Saints   68
    My Dream New Orleans   69
    fat tuesday   71
    Lecture On the Anima   72
    Dream Of John and Yoko   73
    Diamond Sutra   74
    Consecration   76
    An Irish Blessing   79

Enunciation Lessons   81

    Enunciation Lessons   83
    My Lady Copia   85
    Georgia Pines   86
    Gaming the Moon   87
    Do Just It   88
    This Poem   89

Escape Plan	90
Reasons For Dialing 911	91
The Carsitters	92
Schedule Adjustment	94
End Of the Line	95

Immensities   97

Immensities	99
The Paradine Case	100
Galago	101
The Director Is an Idiot	102
The Humanities In Space	104
My Dream Tucson	106
The Rollerbladers At 3 AM	107
I Dreamed I Had Three Different Houses	108
American Dream	109
My Celebrity Dreams	110
My Mars Dream	114
About the Author	115

Acknowledgments

My thanks to the editors of the following journals and e-zines where some of the poems previously appeared.

"American Dream," "Pathways," "Woman At The Kroger," *Bird's Eye Review*; "3 Failed Transactions," *Chicken Pinata*; "Lecture On The Anima," *Conversation Poetry Quarterly*; "Blood Sacrifice," "Homunculus," *Danse Macabre*; "Galago," "My Dream Tucson," and "I Dreamed I Had Three Different Houses," *Liebamour*; "My Celebrity Dreams," *Dream People*; "Dog's Body," "Do Just It," "My Mars Dream," "Five Reasons My Dream Of Tucson Was Impossible," *Good-Time Emporium*; "Back There," "Stendahl's Mirror," *Honey Land Review*; "Gaming The Moon," "Men Of Thor," *Lunarosity*; "Homecoming Flood," *Menagerie*; "Immensities," "To A Former Brother-In-Law," *Online Whispers & [Shouts]*; "Escape Plan," *Penny Ante Feud*; "An Irish Blessing," "My Lady Copia," *Qarrtsiluni*; "Fat Tuesday," "My Lost Years: The Sonnet," *Rhythm*; "First Memory," "Katie O," "Primal," *Sleet*; "The Bear," "End Of The Line," "The House At The Bottom Of The Lake," *Tangent*; "A Flower," "I Wish You Many Bats," "My Dream New Orleans," *Words-Myth*.

"I Wish You Many Bats" was written for the wedding of Laurie Montgomery and Gary Olson.

The Northrop Frye quotation used as head note to the poem "Consecration" is from *The Educated Imagination* (Indiana UP, 1964).

I am indebted to the suggestions of many editors over the past two years. In particular, I would like to thank three: Graham Burchell of Words-Myth, David Nettleingham of the Conversation Paperpress and *Conversation Poetry Quarterly*, and Susan Bright of Plain View Press.

Many of my colleagues at Life University have offered their encouragement, particularly David Wallace and Rebekah Janiak of the General Education Department. Thanks to Lakmal Siriwardana for his dudesmanship and technical help.

Thanks also to my parents and my brothers and sisters, who all show up in my dreams in one way or another.

Finally, my love and thanks to my daughter Ada, always my greatest teacher.

Pathways

Pathways

I was telling my brother how I used to pick up an old trail
near our house. It led through the suburbs, lawn to lawn,
had to be divined in places. But the trees gradually multiplied
until they revealed a woodland path that led all the way
down to the river.

From the banks, it was a short wade out to an island
hidden in pines. How many times had I visited there!
On the north side, no more sign of life than an occasional
outbuilding. But to the west, a road leading through the ruins
of a once-thriving resort community.

Hearing the details, my brother frowned. *Where was this?*

Then I was telling my father how before I had a car and worked
at the credit union downtown, I would sometimes take an old ferry
—no larger than a skiff. I would walk down the hill
to the Mississippi, take off my shoes and socks, and join the line
of yawning commuters.

There were pathways here too, skirting the river on both sides.
And if the day were bright enough, I often preferred to jog home
through the archways of trees, which muffled the traffic sounds
from the highway.

Was this in Minneapolis or St. Paul? my father asked, confused.

The better part of my life is spent in dreams.
Only by chance awakenings do I learn where I have been.

First Memory

My brother Tim is in the backyard.
He is slowly chewing Milk Duds
from a theatre-size box.

It is unusual for him not to automatically
share with his younger brother,
since such treats are rare,

but this one is just for him. I stare in
fascination at his scabbed face
as I continue to turn the

strange phrase *hit by a car* around
in my head. But I have no desire
to share with him or to test

for the brother underneath all that
monster makeup. In fact, I am
feeling self-conscious, unsettled by

the whole broken routine of the day,
the neighbor girl's tearful story,
my mother's mad dash out the door,

the phone ringing with each new report,
my lost nap.

Primal

Scent of plum blossoms along the parkway.
A lunch box: warm milk, Miracle Whip.
Rubber raincoats, green beans from the garden.
Bath beads, chlorine from the pool next door.
A dead squirrel. Cigarette smoke soaked into
your grandparents' furniture.

Sounds of summer through the screen window.
Planes circling in landing patterns overhead.
Doors banging, kitchen radio, cookie jar lid.
The tub draining like a giant slurping a straw.
A dog barking down the street, roaming free
in an era before leash laws.

Sight of cars passing below the footbridge.
Lawns like prairies of weeds and wildflowers.
Green glass, hippie fashions, backyard fires.
A balloon released into the sky. Car tracks
neatly etched into snow. A bat getting in
through the open skylight.

Brittle texture of leaves in the window well.
New tar in the street snapping like taffy.
Raised bumps on corn, slickness of the peels.
The smooth hull of an aluminum canoe.
The humidity of a warming house, and
pinch of parent-laced skates.

Taste of bananas back then, more mango-y.
Christmas cookies, anise, and rhubarb pie.
Icicles tasting slightly of mitten, your appetite
always racing on a cold day. Salt and butter.
Bitter things not for putting into the mouth:
grass, twigs, dandelions.

The first pictures forming in your head as
you read. How slowly the Mummy walked,

but always caught up with you. Dark boxes
in the basement. Nights you stirred in sleep,
dreaming of superpowers, and knocked all
the bedclothes to the floor.

The House At the Bottom Of the Lake

One afternoon, I caught a glimpse of roof near the deepest part
of the lake. Grandpa told us the story: how *unscrupulous movers*
risked a short cut, got stuck in snow until the ice cracked through.
It hadn't taken long, then, for the house to list and sink.

I lay back in the boat that summer day and imagined the rest
from what I had seen, thrilled to realize that the waters we fished
for sunnies could contain such secrets. And then to contemplate
the weight of the loss, the family deprived of a home. For I was
quite young, had no trouble imagining the once-bright kitchen,
the children's rooms, the kids who had lost their treasures. Had
they floated over the site the next spring, peered down sadly
into their own reflections?

More than that: the lake bottom itself was now revealed to me.
Reeds grew everywhere around the house like unmowed grass.
Fish nested in the closets, water sluiced down staircases, chairs
floated up from the floors. This was my jar placed in Tennessee:
my entrée into depths running further than I could see.

Men Of Thor

After Sunday morning church came the second worship service.
And you watched transfixed while two teams in armature clashed,

maybe wearing your knock-off jersey, or clutching the football
you would toss around with your brother during halftime outside,

where it would gain a thin coat of ice and turn into a hard shell.
But you had your gloves, which you took on and off to throw,

and you were proud to share your cold with warm-weather teams
from Texas or California, to see visiting players discompose,

and you were sorry when the Super Bowl became a fast track
in New Orleans or Pasadena because you were the winter warriors,

with players like Page and Eller and Siemon, who smashed through
blockers while their silent coach chewed gum on the sidelines.

And when the other teams from the North like the Chicago Bears
or the Green Bay Packers showed up, a true battle would ensue,

with your players dressed like purple superheroes, and the offense
firmly standing its ground, White and Yary and Tingelhoff,

and Tarkenton would dance around like a man on fire until he found
his receiver, lobbing the ball to Chuck Foreman or John Gilliam,

as you lay on the floor head in hands, feeling each handoff in your
gut and gritting teeth while each pass was in the air, a possibility,

and the referees would bring out the chains for a measurement, but
the field would turn into mud and snow, with white lines invisible,

and even though male reticence was a hard rule, these players were men who were like boys, always excitable and emotional in victory.

When the game ended, you would face a long week of school and early-evening darkness. Until finally it was Sunday afternoon again,

and an announcer's voice would break your vigil, and the TV would become a kind of hearth, spreading its light outward and everywhere.

My Lost Years: The Sonnet

The Linden Hills mansion, the duplex in St. Paul
half a dozen housemates, forgotten now.
Working odd hours in a Mexican restaurant
bonding with coworkers, but remaining apart.
Riding the busses along Selby-Lake
dreaming of escapes to a warm-weather place.
A two-month road trip, a dubious lost love,
fatigues, strange haircut, fancying myself a punk.
At one point, the program for teacher certification
I dropped out of, indifferent to failing.

So much of this period is now a blur:
I recall no homecomings, only departures.
Thrift stores, cigarettes, the reliable sense of angst
I could count on to delay becoming a man.

My Dream Of Mill Valley

The station wagon pulled up to
a large house, yellow and angular.
Huge train engine in front with a cartoon face.
A sign read, *Pool*.

The conversation in the car about property value continued.
A million, said one.
Two million, I suggested, knowing even in my dream
that it wasn't enough.

My father was there, myself, my brothers and sisters,
young as they had always looked to me.
In the back seat,
my former sister-in-law from Tiberon.

I was explaining to my sister Amy
how I had commuted on the Golden Gate Express
while the former sister-in-law
frowned steadily at my every word.

A German man bustled up to the car,
beaming, his hair a bouncing forelock.
He offered us sausage, and, seeing my father hesitate,
said, *It's good food*.

My father, the same age as me now,
began to mumble that we had already eaten,
but saw the shake of the man's head,
and his lips form the words NO DEAL.

And so we all tumbled out of the car.
I took a moment to breathe in
the glowing California day,
just starting to recede into dusk.

Inside the kitchen, a kid's paradise

of twin beds, toys, and Lego benches.
My brothers and sisters sat down to eat,
to a small sausage neatly sliced into cubes.

I cupped my small portion in my hand,
started to put it into my mouth.
Amy said, *I want one, too.*
I said, *I'll get yours later*, eating first.

For clearly I was meant to be
a partaker at this feast,
no longer as old as my father,
no longer even vegetarian.

How very strange it all was,
my dream of Mill Valley!
But I had visited there while young,
and had to be young to return.

To a Former Brother-In-Law

I imagine myself in a Las Vegas motel near where your wedding reception will be. I'm in a small room, not part of a blocked-off suite. The air conditioning doesn't work. Out in the courtyard, the pool is marsh green in the desert sun. I check my clothes: rumpled shirt, nice pants mysteriously grass-stained, as if from one of our football games.

I think of the card I would like to send to you, and what I would like to write on it. *I understand why you can't invite me to your wedding—of course I wouldn't want to make anyone uncomfortable*, I begin, but that sounds like complaining. *We were brothers*, I start again, but that is too over-the-top. I could lead in with a fifty-dollar bill and "Best Wishes to You Both," although I realize I will probably never meet the bride.

I recall our jokes and Spinal Tap accents. The cruises down the Strip, nickel slots, and errand-running for cigarettes. Escapes from the family as it became mired down in holidays and in-fighting. And I wonder if, in the bottom corner of the card, where such endearments are not out of place, there might be room for a rough but legible *Love You, Man*.

Three Failed Transactions

1.
Back in Tucson, I find myself
the sole owner of the lot on Drachman Street.
I go around back to check on the old guest house.
It is still there, the size of a one-car garage.
I sort through an enormous ring of keys
before finding the one I want.

I enter, noticing small pools of water on the floor,
other signs of neglect. I cross to the bed,
feel how soft it is, and sit down.
There are magazines on the bedside stand,
but I cannot read the covers
or tell how long they've lain there.

Abruptly, a man wearing a Disney Pluto costume
enters the house, singing,
back from his job at a children's party.
He sees me and removes the jowly felt head,
revealing a bald man of perhaps fifty underneath.
I then notice a few potted trees and furnishings.

He is clearly a squatter, and I deserve to be paid.
So I sit down to sign him up, officiously,
throwing in some wherefores and parties of the first parts
while the man sweats over the rent, offering just $35 a week.
Surprised, I look up from my scrawling at his tired face,
sensing that he has offered all he can pay.

2.
The scene around me shifts.
I am approached by a former colleague, Danielle,
who had once been deserted by her husband for a year.
She starts to tell me of her renewed sufferings,
how her brother thinks her husband still a jerk,
how this time she is determined to leave him.

An agreement falls into place: we will become a family,
myself, Danielle, and her two daughters. I'm so close
to her I can almost touch her sad face
—then she is gone.

3.
I am now at a bank located in a store
being handed a slip requesting 51 dollars cash back
by a well-to-do businessman, who is in no hurry.
I have to leave him for the drive-through,
where I search on the ring for another key
to unlock Sheryl's drawer.

She is not in today, and the man is a regular customer,
disappointed at not to be able to flirt with her.
I look along the long line of drawers for Sheryl's,
instantly unlock it with the first key I try,
then begin to search for the bills.

Two twenties, one ten. I find a single bill
at the bottom of a bound-up stack.
When I count out the cash to the waiting man,
I realize it must have come from a bundle
to be retired. It is barely legible, frayed,
worn down almost to black and white.

I apologize to him and head back to the till,
deciding to make up the difference in quarters.
Scooping some coins out of the tray,
I notice that one is quite unusual,
resembling an old Liberty head dollar
but gleaming like a polished bronze plate.

As I turn the coin over a couple of times,
it appears to sprout wings. I hold it up, remarking,
It looks like an amulet to be worn around one's neck.
At a back table, two little girls are watching us,
sitting solemnly at a table with their mother,
whose face I am unable to discern.

One girl has dark hair, one light. The blonde girl
asks to see the dollar, asking, *Ooh, is that money?*
I look again at the coins: the winged one has
come alive in my hand. The other is a golden ornament
with a twisted coral pattern at the top
and sparkling sapphire and garnet highlights.

Yes, I lecture to the girl. *This coin represents
the Western continent, with its churning Arctic seas.
On the winged coin is a wise goddess of Eurasia.
You each must have one.* I hand over the coins,
ignoring the well-to-do man and my responsibilities.
True, I have mismanaged money, but there are deeper tributes
to be paid.

Five Reasons My Dream Of Tucson Was Impossible

The rain was pervasive,
awakening a jungle undergrowth
that invaded my guest house,
suddenly recalled to mind for its
close quarters. The fetid air
did not smell clean,
like mesquite.

Sixth Street looking like Monopoly houses
in a row, the perspective all wrong.
The streets narrowed for dream travel,
a dark sky arching its belly
overhead. Not the right sort
of clarity for nighttime:
no stars.

A car pulling up for the softball team.
Duane, my dissertation director,
angry at my missing so many years of games.
We were going away to play
at Sports Park, at night,
while the thunder rumbled
its foreshadowing.

Vast expanse of highway,
mountains in the distance,
sudden reprieve of the wide desert sky.
No other cars, no job to commute to,
no child. That was all right
for grad school, but distinctly outré
even for a dream.

Unbidden, I heard myself
calling my daughter's name,
Ada Luisa, Ada Luisa,
giving it a Spanish inflection.
And in that moment I felt her presence,
asleep in the next room,
secreted away like
a roadside shrine.

Homecoming Flood

There is a thunderstorm predicted as I return from a trip,
and the air of something unsettled.

I walk around back, where a tribe of Lost Boys is encamped
by the soccer net.

Formerly the span of an arm, the brook now resembles
the Mississippi of my youth.

Muddy shoals form a border on one side, and a peninsula
juts out into the rushing water.

I return to check on my young daughter, who is excited,
seeing the damage and awaiting my return.

The storm resumes, so her mother leaves quickly, before
all of the roads are blocked.

Together, the two of us watch at the window while the rain
starts over and erases.

Animal Myths

Animal Myths

Crows fly in unwavering lines,
snakes eventually go blind,
and elephants trot off to die.

Fish can shut their eyes to sleep
crocodiles forlornly weep
and moles can sort of see.

The eel has two beating hearts
barn mice grow up into rats
and birds listen for worms.

Worms turn into lightning bugs
bears give suffocating hugs,
and hippos sweat real blood.

Running horses stay aground,
honest men could once be found
who'd never put another down.

A Flower

We were not present at that marriage
of functionality to essence, nor witness
to the original sequence which might
have induced *Archaefructus* to curl
its leaves upward to form the first
fragrant cupola. Petals emerged,
delicate as flypaper, to dust primitive
legs and wings. And much later color,
kaleidoscopic to the compound eye.
Nectar: sweet but sticky landing strip.
Blooms: top-heavy, swaying, hypnotic.
It was not for us that the flower came
into being. Not for us to perceive one as
beautiful, not for a hundred million years.

The Bear

I've wasted much time trying to retrain the body,
treating it like a bear cub: *No, you can't have that.
Slow down a minute, Hoss.* I get it to sleep when
it wants to stay up, push it away from table before
it's had its fill, make it stay active when it wants
to escape from labor, or just retreat into its cave.

But it, too, has a will of its own, insisting I take
dictation while it mumbles on in animal syntax,
half-in, half-out of winter dreams. And I've learned
(over the years) to relent in my quest for constant
vigilance, to let the bear forage on its own for awhile.
I wonder: *Where is it going? What does it know?*

The Earth Witch

It is the right time of year to search for the Earth Witch. I once found her lair. It is past the subdivision with its orbit of builders' waste and tires. Past a ring where teens toss beer cans and cats abandon their litters. Past a fisherman's trail, where two lawn chairs face each other, holding a conversation in the woods. Beyond the green briars curling from the soil like cruel whips. At the lakeshore, you get the feeling of being watched. Time is remote–you can feel the swell of the earth. I once spotted tall figures walking along the far shore. It was the Crane People. I watched them awhile in silence, until early darkness surprised me. So I cut across the thickest part of the woods, parting vines with a stick. Then the forest opened up to me. Just ahead, an ancient oak stood covered in ciphers. A zigzag arrow: snake. Eight-rayed circle: spider. Many Xs and markings I can no longer recall. Hanging from the branches were knotted cords of small skulls–opossum, rabbit, skunk. I crossed over a circle of stones blackened by ceremonial fire. Stepping quietly, knowing an Earth Witch had received her visions here–once, long ago.

Back There

There's an old tree in that lot where a Divorced Man stood a long time,
waiting for his estranged children to return. Beneath it are two bikes,
a girl's and a boy's, now rusted out. Those skid marks on the road
mark the spot where a Teenage Girl followed another car too closely.
There used to be a small shrine and a pot of flowers to mark the spot.
That obelisk is what's left of a sign pole—some recollect a gas station
or a fruit stand—and a little further beyond, by the bend in the creek,
are the ruins of a campground, where the faithful once gathered
to perform baptisms. Deeper into the woods is an abandoned bus
with *Community Baptist* in faded lettering on the side. It's said
a Wild Boy left behind at a meeting once made it his home. You see
traces of his campfire on the nearby charred stones. By the shore,
there is a turned-over boat with a hole in the hull left by fishermen
and plastic bait cups that never degrade. The foxes used to be plentiful.
It still pays to be on your guard against snakes. A huge pyramid
of tires stacked on pallets looks like a monument to a lost civilization.
You come upon it suddenly after parting the Tarzan vines of kudzu.
Those old boards jutting from the tulip tree are a hunter's blinds.
That granite formation resembling a woman's head is the Sad Lady,
who heard voices and abandoned her family one spring. The irises
that grow near were planted by her children, who mourned her loss,
even after she was eventually found and taken home. Watch out for
the boarded-up well near the chimney stone of the sharecropper's shack.
Occasionally, a curious dog sniffs around the site before the bottom
drops out of its day. Soon its memory is displaced by another pet,
and the *LOST* signs on the utility poles are reduced to staples and pulp.

Dog's Body

Perhaps the children had wanted to help,
For the grave had not been dug too deep.

Or the hard clay had proved too difficult a test,
so a bier of leaves and twigs had finished the job.

After the downpour, the skull lay exposed,
big as a sloth's, the cruel looking incisors

lapping the jaw. A piece of fuzz clung
to one eye socket, adding a touch of Groucho,

while the body curled underneath in a parody
of hearth and sleep. One hard paw pushed

upward through the soil. The smell was ghastly.
And so my daughter and I retrace our steps,

our hike to the creek postponed. She is full
of questions, though, curious to know the breed.

Perhaps a German shepherd or retriever, I answer.
Maybe a shepherd, she says, looking disturbed.

Why did they leave it there, Daddy?
The rain uncovered the body. Nobody's fault.

Will they come back to check on it?
It's hard to say. The mud bank just washed away.

I don't like to walk down that road anymore.
It'll be O.K. I can come back with the shovel.

Will you bury it? Yes. It was someone's pet.
Will it stay buried this time? I'll make sure.

Does she think we should come back then and

leave flowers? A bit hesitantly, she says *Yes–*

I guess–if it was someone's pet. The crisis
in the past, I reach out to take her hand.

Stendhal's Mirror

two white-tailed deer
cross the dirt road

one just a fawn,
the other its mother
—
the fawn hides its neck
in the bush

the doe stands in profile,
not moving until I pass
—
the Chinese thought deer
signaled the nearby presence
of immortals
—
as I enter the subdivision,
noise of a Bobcat engine
—
the sound loud enough
to scare into silence
the schipperke

that generally barks
as it guards
its yard
—
from down the street,
shouts of Hispanic landscapers
become more melodic
—
preschoolers playing in a garage

their intensity suggests
they've been up
for hours

—
sugar maples and oaks,
leaves so green
they appear plastic

magnolia and hydrangea blooms
overripe in august
—
odor I mistake for fertilizer
coming from the corner

and then that cliché:
the unmistakable smell of death
—
a snug white sheet
held down by cinder blocks,
covering the remains
of a very large animal

miasma of gnats circling overhead
—
buzzing of cicadas in the trees,
now, with the noise of morning traffic,
just about reaching a standoff
—
garbage truck speeding
along its route, customers
many houses apart
—
For Sale signs listing
commercial contacts
or financial companies

foreclosures,
hidden tragedies

butterfly the color of coneflowers,
discovering an exotic species
of like purple
to hide in

city vehicle passing
on the wrong side of the road

from a porch somewhere
an adult baritone
reassuring a child:
It's probably here for the deer

the driver complaining to me,
One a yer neighbors
must a been drivin pretty fast
to hit a dang deer

I tell him I've seen mother and fawn
earlier this day, point to where

he spits in consternation,
repeats his observation

old man from down the block
bounding proudly uphill
with his wife

he points to the hollow and remarks,
They come up out of there all the time!"

if I stay any longer with these others,
I know I will have trouble
seeing things as they are

———

famous definition of a novel:
a mirror walking along the road

———

had I not seen the doe and fawn,
many ill omens today

had I not seen the dead deer,
perhaps only a pleasant ramble.

Rainforest Honeymoon

This was to have been a working honeymoon.
The two of us were staying at an Amazon resort.
You asked me to bring you back some soap.
In the lobby, I was helped into my all-red uniform,
looking somewhat like a tree frog. For you,
I stopped at a market stall and pocketed one of the
packages, apple-scented, half red and half green.
I then set off to explore before my shift began,
abandoning the atrium, observing the uneasy
integration of commercial stalls and real jungle.

I ended up in an unused corridor, far away.
The iguanas had reclaimed the terrain.
They were poised on the branches, silent.
I pondered the strangeness of no longer being single.

The Truth About Lemmings

White Wilderness, 1958

To get the lemmings, for this area of Alberta was unpopulated, the filmmakers had to buy pets from Inuit children in Manitoba and airlift them in. But these were placid creatures, naturally, and needed to be shooed and chased to perform at all. For the frantic "migration scene," a lazy susan was brought in and the lemmings were spun while the camera moved in for a tight shot on their faces. Our narrator Winston Hibbler speaks these lines: *A kind of compulsion seizes each tiny rodent and, carried along by an unreasoning hysteria, each falls into step for a march that will take them to a strange destiny.* Then the filmmakers cut, for it was time for a second piece of Disney magic. The animals were wrangled and brought to a river where two camera set-ups awaited. One, to capture the lemming approach to the "ocean." Another, to record the mythical "suicide plunge." Hibbler lies to us again: *As they approach the sea, they've become victims of an obsession—a one-track thought: Move on! Move on!* Buried in these words, you can practically hear the hurry-ups of the production crew. And so the lemmings took the plunge, just as scripted, although there is nothing suicidal in the nature of the species. In fact, some refused to cooperate in this scene at all, had to be grabbed by PAs and lobbed like hand grenades over the embankment, while the all-knowing Hibbler intones, *This is the last chance to turn back. Yet over they go, casting themselves out bodily into space!* Cut. Cut!—really, this ought to be enough True Life Adventure for any family's Sunday night entertainment. Yet as the camera zooms in for its final requiem upon the scene, it does capture an important fact or two. Fact One: lemmings are, clearly, only novice swimmers. Fact Two: placed into an unexpected struggle for life, these ones will not last.

A Dictionary Of Animal Symbols

Ape, Vanity, Imitation

Ape was always other,
our tag-along brother.

Painters tried to blame
him for original sin
by placing an apple
in his mouth.

Fortunately for us,
the ape could not thus
protest his own
innocence.

Bear, Ancestry, Prophecy

Sleeping under a bearskin
at night will summon
dark dreams.

Wearing a bear mask
emboldens one to address
forest familiars.

Bear is the guise shamans
put on to see what
lies ahead.

Bee, Diligence, Duty

Essene priests were said
to buzz about the hive
of the Church.

Sweet is the path of belief,
but so often marked
with nettles.

Boar, Ferocity, Courage

When the battle grows thick,
send in the helmeted boars!

They will scrum with gusto
and root out the very demons
from the soil. Yes,

when the sides are picked,
I bet on the boars.

Bull, Potency, Life-force

To seize the bull's horns
is to seize the day,
to rush bellowing
into that good night,

not to dodge one's desires
with the usual feints
and ruses.

For the victor:
a shower in bull's blood.

Camel, Stoicism, Sobriety

The camel picks itself up
and dusts itself off,

ceases its complaining
and shoulders its burden,

always understanding that
its life-journey is not easy,

and no drinks will be served.

Coyote, Resourcefulness, Mischief

A coyote can rearrange
a campsite quickly
by dragging off supplies
in its teeth.

If chastised, it will
retreat, tongue lolling
in a panting grin.

Pursuit is pointless.

Crocodile, Ill-temper, Destruction

A crocodile sets traps
in its teeth and appears,
to all the world,
to be asleep.

Egyptian gods were fond
of borrowing its jaws
to eat out the hearts
of enemies.

Dolphin, Transformation, Playfulness

What do you do
with a drunken sailor?
Perhaps turn him
into a dolphin.

So Bacchus did,
before casting
his new play-mate
upon the jaunty waves.

Donkey, Humility, Obstinacy

Jesus indeed chose a lean
machine, though he might have
needed a tow.

When stuck in the mud, this
no-frills ride might just decide
not to go.

Dove, Peace, Love

Doves are born in the throats
of martyrs, become moans in
the mouths of lovers, and are
then swallowed by politicians,
who close their lips to all hope.

Elephant, Chastity, Longevity

The bull elephant was said
to remain chaste for his mate
and to stay at her side for life.

True, to hide an indiscretion
would be quite a feat.

Goat, Lust, Devil

I have tested the
devil-bearded one,
heard stories

of kicking hooves
bringing about
great destruction,

of vile lust, and

of orneriness raised
to metaphysical rage,

yet always found him
kin to lamb. So let us
praise the goat.

Hedgehog, Ingenuity, Gluttony

The hedgehog rolls
into a ball, knocking its food
from the vine.

It then skewers the fruit
like a true gourmand,
on its bristly behind.

Horse, River, Sun

The flow of a horse
is its mane.

A running horse
is relentless,
hooves barely
touching the soil.

A wild horse
rearing in silhouette
is suddenly
outlined in light.

Lynx, Vigilance, Vision

The lynx is acute
on a stakeout,
pacing patiently,
its coat of spots
apt camouflage,

its eyes two
penetrating beams.

It can tail a suspect
over snow and ice,
paws padded
for stealth, until
muscles tense,
and kit moves in
for the kill.

Owl, Wisdom, Death

Who
would wish to see
what an owl sees at night?

What
graveyard goings-on,
what plots of men and mice?

Where
forest kills are common,
and whatever is, is right?

Peacock, Immortality, Pride

Vision of the divine,
hundred-eyed beauty
praised as immortal,
the peacock has sipped
from a golden chalice
it chooses not to share.

Snake, Power, Deceit

A coiled snake
generates its own
electricity.

it can swallow
the whole earth,
or feast on its
own tail.

it can stretch out
like lightning,
then dissemble
and be gone.

Stag, Tree, Vitality

The stag grows
new branches
each Spring,

and magically
finds its way
to healing herbs.

It is said to be
a favorite of fairies.

Tiger, Royalty, Danger

He who dares
ride a tiger
had better be a god.

Otherwise,
the tiger decides
who lives or dies.

Toad, Moon, Witch

The bulge of a toad's
throat is the moon,
and inside its head

a night-jewel.

A toad lives
in middle-earth
and only comes out
in foul weather.

Its lip is curled from
the poison it brews.

Vulture, Gatekeeper, Aging

Vultures are forever
present at both ends:
as protective mothers,
as hasteners of decay.

Necessarily, so the cycle
can play itself out again.

Whale, Rite of Passage, Rebirth

A whale makes a most
pleasant accommodation,

where one may wait out
dark phases of the moon.

One may tap its fine teeth
with a hammer, or spelunk

around its ample belly—
looking forward, of course,

to ultimate deliverance.

I Wish You Many Bats

A Chinese Blessing for My Sister

I wish you many bats.

I wish you upside-down bats: *happiness has arrived*.
I wish you bats with peaches: long life, joy in each other.
I wish you bats with catfish: the joy carried over year to year.

I wish you two bats, for *double good fortune* on your wedding day.
I wish you five bats, for your continued health, perseverance,
success, kindness, and course of life with nature.
Five bats with a shou character for longevity.
Five bats with a box to ensure peace and harmony.

Red bats, the color of your child's hair, for your immense love.
Bats against a red sky, that your hopes for him may soar.
Many bats with heavenly clouds and many bats with coins.

May each bat be captured so that you may retain all joys.
May each bat have a musical stone in its mouth at your celebration.

Ghosts

Ghosts

The optics of cathedral ceilings.
Shadows in the stairwell.
Humidity streaking an upstairs pane.
Furniture, indented by former occupants,
loosely shrouded in dust covers.
A draft against the window curtain.
Smoke-wreaths.

The spirit of a place, its *genius loci*.
The pathetic fallacy.
First impressions, left by strangers,
of whom the matter is forgotten.
Every hateful act of a lifetime
coming back, coming back.
The wraiths of our regrets.

Dream After *Rashomon*

The Woman
walks ahead on the woodland trail

in her hiking shorts,
backpack firmly affixed like a cocoon.

The Man
follows a few paces back,

dragging two wooden kitchen chairs,
carrying a smaller pack around his neck.

The trail grows rockier, starts a steep descent,
and the man gives up in frustration,

leaving the chairs behind.
Feeling sympathetic,

I do my best to add them to
my own burden, but have to give up, too.

The Man looks sheepish,
but not ungrateful for my efforts.

The Woman stands scornful,
wading out into a stream to cool her feet.

All men love lederhosen,
she says, with firm conviction.

I start to contradict her,
recalling a childhood friend to mind.

All men love lederhosen,
she repeats,

while small minnows dart in and around
her firmly planted legs

Homunculus

People were playing one of those parlor games about survival
    in a seminar classroom, and the question,
        What would you do if attacked by a giant squid?
            fell to Emily.

She stood up slowly, climbed to the front of the room
            and started lecturing,
    throwing out the name Ruth Benedict,
        then defensively challenging,
           You mean you guys don't know who she is?

She continued on, incoherently. It was now evident to others,
    including her friends, that her thoughts were in disarray.
        One man sitting nearby was mocking her
            — or rather the prompt —
    twirling his fingers in his gloved hand.
        He smashed at them with his other fist
            while his companion laughed.

A little later, I was speaking to my cousin Lilah,
        who had recently learned she was pregnant.
        It was a test-tube baby:
    Lilah had worried that she was past conceiving,
        but now was filled with new love and pride.

Jealous, Emily saw us talking and came over. She announced,
        I found something in my contact-lens solution,
    pulling out what looked like a tiny speck of a person,
        a homunculus,
    fragile and translucent in the sun.
    Then she snapped it away with a flick
            of her fingernail
        and walked off in a huff.

You never do find it again, I mourned—
            that drop of old Gnostic soul.

Eminent Domain

The bulldozers edged into our yard from the lot next door.
They cut across the narrow ridge of the ravine,
dislodging sprinkles of rock and soil.

I walked halfway down the hill to the worksite,
approached the mounds raised by the machines.
A wide crack had opened through the middle of the lawn,
sectioning off half an acre of bottomland.

Shortly, the bulldozers returned and began to fill in
the brook. You couldn't discern it through the narrow
gash in the clay. Alarmed, I waved my arms.

A sleepy-looking man leaned out of his metal cab,
alluded to the months of officially posted signs.
I tried to persuade him I had seen none.

None? he replied, slowly repeating the word.
Across the lawn, a silt fence was already being
stretched into place. It was going to be too late.

Blood Sacrifice

We had escaped a tourist attraction, the World of Corporate America, by running down a escalator and bursting into an interior courtyard. There we learned the great secret: ancient pyramids in North America! First a statue of a puma-god, carved of stone, rose to the third story. Then, just as we were seized by the guards, we saw the monument itself, well preserved, all of adobe. Of course, we knew our lives were forfeit.

But the corporate head, enfeebled with age, sagged as he approached us. I couldn't help taking his arm, which felt light, as though hollowed out. He explained how the headquarters had been founded at the ancient site. Then others who had breached the restricted area were taken up to him, a brown-skinned mother with a son about eight. We saw the boy's look of wonderment and perceived, sadly, that this was a secret no child could keep. We watched as an employee guided him up for a look and out of view. Then she placed his head into a notch on the wall and broke his neck.

The CEO studied our reaction as mother screamed, then was silenced. Apparently our lack of protest pleased him, for he gestured to a second site that had escaped our notice. It was a kind of obelisk, formerly a monument to a native god. It resembled an ibis or a bolt of lightning. A group of pilgrims gathered around it, each wearing a lightning bolt metamorphosed into the company logo. Others had known the secret, then, and lived. We chatted among ourselves nervously, wondering who would be marked for sacrifice, who deemed worthy of the elect.

Frankenstein

As a bearded student, I looked a bit like Victor,
but my hair has receded, revealing more of my face.
Then, I often found myself in the middle of a crowd.
Now, I find it quite difficult to be close to others.
On my face are scars of past illnesses and blows.
My back is stiff, my knees have lost their spring.
My fingers have always seemed the wrong size,
too thick to work small buttons or dials with ease.
I might have kept a lower profile had I been less tall.
I would have preferred that; I am reserved by nature.
In my early years, I was on speaking terms with God.
Now I have chosen to walk through this world alone.
I've come to realize that we are each many selves,
compounded of all of our past loves and mistakes.

I Was Dead:

stone cold, there in the mall, standing as stiff as a mannequin.
The lighting was pale, all the departments were closed, and
a young woman stood next to me, also dead. Kindly, she took
my hand and guided me to the entryway, where it was brighter.
The front door was calmly monitored by a former acquaintance
who recognized her, nodded slightly, and buzzed us through.
By degrees we were becoming less robotic in our movements,
though not yet alive. And we continued down a tapering aisle
through another glass door and another, my recently-deceased
companion waved through by former coworkers and friends.
And I benefited too, though truly I was just along for the ride.
By now we could tell that the next bright gate would be the last,
and beyond it, street traffic and sun. But we were blocked by
a large man in a control booth who shook his head, stubbornly
barring us. Then all hope of leaving the commercial crypt fled,
and everything faded to black. When we came to, we were back
in the store—unable to move, adorned in heavy winter coats.

My Little Murder

I was just out of prison. My victim was a man who mistreated
a girl I had fathered. The gun was where I'd stashed it long ago.
One clean shot—then it was cover-up time. I went on a walk
through a ruined industrial area where I'd latched on with a job.
Hiding places for the weapon were everywhere: in the open pits
or fast-hardening cement. Too obvious. I walked on till I reached
the other side of the complex, then broke through a cluster of trees.
Beyond, a dome-shaped mountain rose from a white seashore.
I took the gun and hurled it as far as I could out into the waves,
then stood there for awhile, hoping to feel a change. Coming back,
I came upon an artist's encampment. He was using found materials
discarded by the factory. I was invited to sit down at table with him
and his twelve followers. Throughout, I pretended to be a person
who had regained his sight after years of blindness. Then the artist
gave me some clay and said I could shape it into anything I wanted.

Zombie Peace

We were zombies together, stiff-legged marching over hills and fields: one people, one purpose, one mind, driven by a powerful urge we could not understand. From our graves we came, or risen from hospital beds, or stepping away from plane crashes and war zones and gangbang back alleys. Newcomers were accepted without regard for country or creed, just as they were: pale teen suicides, blueface drowning victims, the natural deaths. We did not walk too fast for the badly decomposed or maimed. Thus our strange little band continued to increase. We progressed through cornfields and small towns, through the shells of strip malls and deserted cities, ever yearning. Murmuring among ourselves, fixing glazed eyes on the boarded-up stores where we had once shopped, the office centers where we once worked, the gated communities where we once lived separate lives. Now we were on the march, all in this together. We scrounged for new recruits everywhere, as fervently as if we were on a spiritual mission of some kind. Perhaps we were. True, some may have overplayed their part, murmuring *brains, brains,* and frightening small children, but that was all quite passé and unnecessary. We were indomitable: no illness or blow from a shovel could ever break up our ragtag but powerful collective. We had no long-term worries: the world would eventually run short of weapons, and till then each bullet expended only bred more slapstick pacifists like ourselves. Peace, it is thought, must eventually prevail in a hungry, post-zombie world. But who can separate the living from the living dead, so stripped as we all are? And what else is that hunger inside us now, if not love?

Satanic Lunch

In short time, I had to get to work. And in this strange city, who was to say where work was? First Street was the address—First Street.

All in a strange city, I must have exited out the wrong side of a building, gotten off at the wrong stop. And now, in short, I was lost.

For making the wrong stop, this was my reward. To be trapped in a building tangle of oaks and Victorian homes. I was disgruntled—

—for it was no reward, to be trapped thus. I walked on, carrying my briefcase. Ahead of me loomed a deserted house with a sheer drop to the ground.

Carrying my briefcase on ahead, I trespassed up to the second story—from which I spied, on the lawn below, piled cushions and furnishings.

While I trespassed on the second story, a group of young people suddenly appeared in the room. Drama students, in a merry mood. Too late to escape!

The group of young people appeared to include one or two coeds. It was altogether a jolly crew, too preoccupied to notice me.

They frolicked, a jolly crew, and their leader was Captain Jack Sparrow. Then he ordered a long dining table covered, for a ceremony was set to begin.

Then the leader, Captain Jack Sparrow—smiling crazily, as if drugged—chose a victim, producing a surgical knife with which to make his incision.

Smiling crazily—also as if drugged—an actress complied as he made a pass with the wicked knife over her abdomen, as neatly as working a zipper.

The actress then complied as he reached in—pulled something out—and placed it into a metal bowl on the table. A long silence followed, for them.

Then he pulled something out of the bowl. Horrified, I was unable to move as he popped a dark substance into his mouth! Seeing me watching, he grinned.

Horrified, I was yet unable to move. And now the others noticed me and laughed. Their leader bounded over, top hat askew, too detached to care what I had seen.

The others noticed this and laughed again. Standing at the window, I asked—*Behind us is the river, and further, Green Valley. If I follow First Street, will I make it to the university?*

I waited there at the window, askance. *This is The Nineteenth Century,* he replied—*a time of many wonders. You will find a green valley, yes, and there is some talk of building a university.*

This is the Nineteen Century, he had said. But how could this have happened? Still, I couldn't help smiling a little at his double-talk, demented though it was.

For how could any of this have happened? Before I had time to respond, Captain Jack and companions bounded out the window, and were gone—

—all this before I had time to respond. Now no one was left in sight. No bloody organs, just grapes brimming the old bowl.

On impulse, I decided to sample one, too, for there was no one in sight. And soon I was back where I belonged, First Street, now widening and resembling a thoroughfare.

In short time, I would be headed back where I belonged on First Street. But by the front drive of another home, I paused before a pile of boxes and began to sort through them.

There by the front drive of the other home, others joined me in the sorting. I opened boxes upon boxes of curios, buttons, and books.

Still others joined me in the sorting—and then I beheld the butterfly. It was purple, the size of a Japanese fan, weakly lifting its damask wings.

As I beheld the purple butterfly—in that brief moment of rapture—I heard a woman point it out to her companion, who replied to her—*It's dead.*

In that one brief moment of rapture—knowing that I shortly had to get to work—
I had stopped to watch an illusion of life generated by a small puff of wind.

And then, in short, I had to get to work.

Letter To Buffy

I sometimes worry on your behalf because your father is absent most of the time, and though you occasionally get a supernatural assist or a professorial word of advice from Giles, I know that's not the same thing as having a real dad. You've helped me out in that department, by the way. My daughter and I find we have diverged in our tastes now that she has tastes of her own. She's bored with sports, and I can't quite accept vampires that sparkle or dialogue skimmed straight from the soaps. It's true you have waded through your own share of schlock and rubber-faced foes, but at least you always had wit, Buffy, and that kept me awake on the couch when I was taking a break from playing the single dad, only too happy to let you hold the world together for awhile.

A Tapestry of Saints

Woman At the Kroger

following Operation Allied Force

I see her in the produce aisle while I am examining onions.
She pauses at the potatoes, her daughter in tow.
And what a merry child she is, skipping across the polished floor,
attracted to the spotlights reflecting off the neat rows of fruit and vegetables.
Her mother is attractive, cropped black hair, wearing a blue windbreaker
with a tent insignia. Perhaps no less than ten years younger than me,
but looking fatigued. She glances up briefly, shadows outlining her cheeks.
Intuitively, I seem to know her whole history: refugee from the Balkans,
newly flown in from the camps along with the many dozens
sponsored by our local churches. Our eyes meet briefly.
She pulls her hands out of the potato bin and turns them over to show no ring.
Her daughter, the same age as my own, has already turned the corner to the next aisle.
The woman speaks her name sharply: *Ola!*— then a string of Slavic words
I cannot follow. I sense that she in turn could not have understood
the compliment I have been poised to pay her on the child,
so regrettably, say nothing. A second later, the girl peeks her head around
to assure her mother that she is still there, and smiles.
Immediately, the woman pushes the cart ahead without putting anything in it,
as if fearing an unsafe zone at the end of the aisle,
there past the discount bins, and unable to bear the thought of further loss.

Katie O

All the hard rock bands lined up for her funeral—
Hüsker Dü, Soul Asylum, the Jayhawks, others.
A rocker herself, she was remembered for her fine
and fiery spirit. The same toughness I had seen
when she was just a freckled miss, late last child
of an old Irish couple who lived in a stone house
across the street. She and I would circle each other
at the bus stop like boxers, a mixture of boy-girl
taunting and just showing off. One day as I sat
on the front bank of our yard, the sparring turned
affectionate. I called out, *Betcha can't kiss me*.
She was only just out of the tub, loosely wrapped
in a towel, but immediately shot across the street
to embrace me in a half-tackle, half-hug. Then
she pressed her lips against my cheek, hard, as if
to brand me hers forever. Of course I was always
hers, remained so even after my family drifted
out to the suburbs. And the years passed, and she
became a local celebrity, until the day she could
no longer fight off the depression that killed her.
But she had given me a look of triumph, that day,
even as her old mother scolded her–*Katie!* Then
she turned to run home just as quickly as she came,
wild and wet, the towel floating up from her legs
like the bright, unruly hem of an angel's dress.

Katie O'Brien, 1962-1999

That Man

who ministered to the sick and poor,
who threw out the moneychangers,
who said we were all sons of God

I still perceive him beneath all
the layers of text and translation,
miracles and myth that

erased his family, his humanity,
and substituted the polemics
of prophecy fulfilled.

I still perceive him after centuries
of anti-Semitism, popes run amok,
and countless cults of the Apocalypse.

I see him, hear his simple words:
Love your enemy, bless those
who curse you

and feel the power of that injunction,
and realize such forgiveness
is truly divine.

A Tapestry Of Saints

Today I have made my own tapestry of saints. I began with
Lucia, a beauty who once carried her eyes on a platter until
her vision was restored. Then added St. Theresa—passionate,
pierced through by an angel's arrow—because she is said
to summon premonitory dreams. St. Albert, because he was
a great scholar and the teacher of Aquinas. St. Contardus:
a true hippie saint, who accompanied the sick on pilgrimages
and was pleasant to be around (good name for a dog, Contardus).
St. Zita: archetype of the unassuming and introspective person.
St. John the Baptist: my family saint, though sometimes said
to represent separation from family (which is appropriate, too).
St. Matilda: patron saint of banks, public works, and stability.
A blue blood, but gracious enough to help you with your taxes.
Cecilia: patroness of music and creative works. The very saint
to see you through a busy poem like this one. St. Joachim Pater:
a surprise choice really, a low-key saint, but the father of Mary,
hence the patron of all fathers. Lastly, St. Catherine of Sienna,
who cut off her hair to avoid a conventional marriage, found her
own circle of friends, and then began a life of service, working for
world peace and caring for prisoners and the sick. She defied
her parent's wishes, choosing to lead the spiritual life instead.
Not a bad role model, I'd say, for your daughter or for mine.

My Dream New Orleans

We stay in guest lodgings
accessed only by fire escapes
and flower-filled balconies.
Shops line the bottom story.
The quality of the sunlight is white.
The grid of the streets is reversed.
To the west, new casinos
are interpolated from Las Vegas.
To the south, the sea.

To escape the crowd,
I often take a bus there,
motoring past parking lots
and trailers of long-term residents.
I hike past barriers around a jetty
and take up my station on a beach.
Crawfish on the sand, dead fish.
Too cold to swim,
but a window on the world.

Coming back has its rewards:
nighttime, a different city to explore.
A street on the east side
I think of as Bourbon Street
that is strangely out of time.
Rows of trees and 19th century shops,
lamplit. I forage along my route
as strange dishes are held out to me,
bouillabaisse and blackened rice.

The street is dotted with red lights.
I know that the blank fronts
of some buildings hide bordellos.
Occasionally, a French matriarch
motions me over. I have been inside:
a circuit in darkness of lit alcoves

like porch-stops on Halloween,
or stations of the cross.
Women motionless as icons.

I prefer being out on the boulevard,
The tree branches reflecting fingers
of moonlight along St. Charles,
pointing toward jungle-like gardens.
Noises of the marketplace
grow muted, careen off
the sounding boards of mansions,
fading in each rebound until only
the soft voices of ghosts are left.

O my city of the dead.

fat tuesday

louie and henry scat singing with the angels
royal street esplanade their voices echo everywhere
cracked throated warblers the sweet songbirds they're not
but the moon is the moon is the moon is the moon
louie and henry emphysema scat singing
and the bourbon in the bottle mixes sin with the soul
by the levee under bridges down the sidewalk boots jingling
king louie has a stubble beard king henry like a troll
marching steps breaking line keeping time to the singing
which is surly with assertion and all hollowed out of tone
louie's not outshouted tries to drown out the world
henry holds his nostrils clears his head like a conch
then giggling leans over like a stand-up bass
and collapses with a curtsy to the people passing by
and collapses with a curtsy to the people passing by

Lecture On the Anima

We had marched on and taken a beachhead at the sea, blue.
At last, it was time for an immersion. Time to shed my
soldier's uniform and take the plunge! Just below the surface,
a school of yellow fish passed. Then a diver's lost bell-jar
of a helmet, half-buried in the sand. I swam out deeper,
past the point where a safe return seemed likely. At once,
my vision began to clear. I sensed that I must be in holy water.
I could see all the way down to the sunken shrine of a lost
Minoan goddess. That expression carved in white marble—
it might have been a smile or a sneer. Her gaze was gold.
Unconsciously, I kicked my legs and swam even deeper.
I could just touch a trident that flashed in a half-closed hand.

Dream Of John and Yoko

I had not thought back to that place in many years, but in my dream I was there, the small white bungalow and the Seville orange tree, with its appealing-looking fruit too sour to eat, and the soil too hard-baked to absorb water, paradoxically supporting life. And I in my graduate school days just moving in, busily setting up the living room, stacking boxes by the couch where my new wife and I would soon slump in exhaustion, happy never to get up. Playing a John Lennon album to keep myself company, feeling the beautiful arid coolness of that later music. And suddenly feeling a kinship with John himself, knowing his art could never have emerged without a separation. For dreams often attack common knowledge and affirm the contrary: it was Yoko, let us consider, who kept the creative rivalry known as the Beatles going indefinitely. And cozy bungalow or not, my marriage would eventually end too, though not in failure. And so it appeared that this dream was no wistful look back at the past, or even about a place. But John had stood by as a kind guide to tell me that it was O.K., now I could safely shelve a past grief, life wasn't easy, and *Whatever gets you through the night, it's alright, it's alright.*

Diamond Sutra

This I have done.

I have biked toward Diamond Lake,
    in late autumn, with my older brother Tim,
    whose ten-speed has raced around the corner ahead.
    With some effort, I have continued on alone,
    on an old bicycle, a child's.

I have followed the slope of Clinton Avenue past a superette,
    noticed candies and gumball machines
    like dim mementoes behind the glass,
    discovered a cluster of new commercial buildings
    of shining glass and polished stone.

I have recognized shops, a restaurant,
    a drugstore so new it seemed to represent
    a yet-to transpire corporate merger.
    Toward the lake, a large building named the Spire
    shaped like a translucent Hershey's Kiss.

I have walked my bike down a short dirt embankment to a path
    and ridden around the lip of the shoreline.
    I have noticed the lake surface appear to expand,
    gelid and rippleless. Still on my bike,
    I have begun to labor heavily,

Not from the strain of no gears, nor from the exertion itself,
    but out of pure and simple grief. I've thought,
    I have not been back here for too long, too many years.
    And I've sobbed, staring out over the handlebars
    at the shining water.

And I've reflected,
    Had I made this trek sooner, would I have felt more complete?
    Would I have become more truly compassionate?
    No matter that these waters, for all of their beauty,
    are utterly unfamiliar to me;

I have fixed upon them as my source.
>Perhaps not the sentimental cause, but the balm
for all of my suffering. My sobs do not allow me
to dwell in these thoughts for long.
When I awake, I am at peace.

Consecration

Literature, then, is not a dream-world: it's two dreams, a wish-fulfillment dream and an anxiety dream, that are focused together, like a pair of glasses, and become a fully conscious vision.
                                        —Northrop Frye

This was at a religious retreat at a small coastal village.

I had hiked through the mountains and come upon an encampment.
The leader was a Dr. Phil-looking man who led
a group of eligible followers seeking mates.
They floated out there, in the water,
stripped of all their accoutrements.

A woman swam over and asked me what I was looking for.
I mumbled, *A nice girl, I guess.*
She gave a little laugh,
and wading over to a pair of disciples,
hooked one with her arm, and brought her up to me.

I looked into the eyes of Tracey.
We bobbed there in the water, introducing ourselves.
She had mid-length brown hair, wavy.
It was not possible to perceive her submerged body,
but we got to talking.

Tracey was a social studies teacher, a graduate of UNC.
Right then and there we became a couple:
embracing, treading water, and making our plans.
We even befriended another pair,
her friend, and a young man who had swum out with me,

a pre-med student who resembled Walter Kirn.
He was a gallant Southerner, a local,
had been a favorite with the ladies,
had even made an enemy,
a powerful town mayor named Farquhar.

A little later I was searching for Tracey in the long line of couples.
Still-unattached women were turning in some sort of report
to the smiling leader, who remarked that the problem
might have been brevity. One cut-up had written only a brief summary
on the back of a postcard. The others laughed,

hiding their own disappointment in a show of solidarity.
I kept walking down the unbroken line
of newly consecrated couples,
through interior rooms each larger than the last,
not seeing Tracey, her friend, or Walter.

The followers were massing as at one of Reverend Moon's weddings,
but we weren't planning on joining the ceremony!
The four of us, young, well educated,
cynical of all such ceremonials,
were taking a bus and eloping.

I left to look for Walter up and down the cliff path.
I found him at last, t-shirted and hiding in a cardboard box.
He told me that in truth,
he had no money for medical school
and couldn't support Tracey.

Tracey is my bride, I corrected him,
and he looked at me kind of oddly.
I couldn't pull him away from there
and so left to find the others.
Getting dark now: the sea had turned choppy.

No sign of the women on the village street.
I had a premonition about Walter,
returned to the site of his shame, but he was gone.
Just a nest of fetal rats in the debris
and my own forebodings.

He's suicidal, I thought. *Gone to do himself harm.*
And I did what I thought I had to do:
I approached the wicked Farquhar's den.

Farquhar, a fortyish blond man,
turned out not to be so bad.
He strolled with me, muttering irritably
about young Walter and his recklessness,
yet not without affection.

Could this be Walter's father? I wondered.
But this was a dream, and there were no answers.

We came to a rocky parapet
just as a cardboard box slid over the edge.
Someone was pounding at the box from inside
with the desperation of one sealed in a casket too soon.
Probably our man Walter.

A splash, and then, defying physical law, the box sunk immediately.
Farquhar and I gazed briefly at each other.
A good sport, he made to take off his jacket,
but then looked relieved, seeing me prepared to jump.
He was more bluster than action after all, was Farquhar.

And so my dream that began in water
returned to water, too. And I took that plunge to rescue
a young man escaping his worries and his bride.
No sworn enemies, only those of his creation,
stouthearted but confused.

And I have no idea if I ever found that box,
or how much of myself might have been in it.

An Irish Blessing

for my father

May the Lord put you in a witness protection program where the Devil can't find you. May you always find yourself in the flow of traffic, and may the slower drivers stay the hell out of your way. May your hair remain red enough to refract harmful UV rays. May your appetite be hearty and the waistband of your trousers slack. May there be no household project to ever get the better of you. May you shit out the colon cancer if it starts to grow back, and then may the doctors go broke trying to find anything else wrong with you. May the church parishioners listen in rapt attention to your readings, and your grandchildren hear your stories without any fidgeting. May you grow just absent-minded enough to forget cross words. May your buddies from Korea stay out of the obituaries. May your partner be there to chide you if you start to become morbid. May you find samples at every supermarket and long-lost treasures at every yard sale. May your coffin be constructed of toothpicks from fine dinners you haven't eaten yet. May winter cold melt in your breath. May the road ahead be soft enough for slippers, and may the Good Lord reserve for you a fine pair of size thirteens.

Enunciation Lessons

Enunciation Lessons

A sad scene in the cell block,
where the inmate hissed.
He did not obey,
and knew the pain of jail.

Many a feud has begun in a pew,
and still more over beauty.
Beaus roam, or grow old.
Some are all talk.

At the hearth, the sergeant offered his memoirs.
A Caesar deceiving women,
pretty nymphs in breeches.
It was an ill hymnal for the English.

A righteous question of philosophy?
Don't laugh. You must persuade the choir!
Zeno is, lives.

Too often in our blindness,
we forget loving-kindness.

To become more socially conscious
of the ocean:
an issue for our nation.
Sure, it makes you nauseous.

The wolf was full and could eat no more:
one cow, with sauerkraut.
A leopard, a second heifer, feathers.
And one oily boy.

Try to show more passion than a machine!

I heard her sing once at the Tongue Bank.
It's located at the junction.
If you linger, watch for cankers.

The chorus was piqued.
It was the end of an epoch,
and the pack had been conquered.

My Lady Copia

Perhaps because I can get so tongue-tied, I am not naturally economical in writing. *Cut half of what you write*, advises my father, who is something of a raconteur. *Drop your last paragraph to avoid appearing argumentative*, counsels my lawyer, himself a gladiator. True, E.B. White held a good school. The English language is naturally redundant: "to be" constructions, excessive nominalizations, clichés—all deservedly banished from the Republic of Letters. Adjectives and figures of speech: never use when an action word will do. And by god, throw away your thesaurus.

It is always surprising, though, when the Occam's Razor falls on poetry: *We cannot consider poems of more than twenty lines. We ask that you kindly sum things up and get to the point.* Of course the poem itself may have been the point: the vent, the spill, the tendril, the brave search party sent out after other words. (Pardon my pleonasm.) The safest course is to unloose the diction only when it's certain to seem appropriate. A eulogy? You can get away with that sort of thing. Trash-talking with friends? Of course you must play that game. An affectionate letter? Even those I have been encouraged to tone down. Don't pontificate, don't come on too strong, don't jinx things with your exuberance. So I end here. It is, as they say, a wrap. *Ad Finem. Vale.*

Georgia Pines

Names like short leaf and loblolly miss
these crocodile ladders, suburban outliers,
ancients in our midst.

Heads above the rest, trunks like torches,
needles flensing sun. Good cactus people
standing their ground.

Wind-brittle, jettisoning intermittent limbs.
Desert-layers, festooning communities
with coniferous strew.

Woodpecker-bored, lightning-struck, bent
like drinking straws: wearing many scars.
Jolly old tars they are,

yet redolent with youth. Lasting for ages
while we are just passing through.

Gaming the Moon

Remember four a.m.—The hour of animation, of wind-fulfillment. Over the dome of the night, a sheet music of sharps. The last of the Christmas lights, unplugged.

My held-out arms: tubular, luminescent. Turn-a-corner, I'll race you. Spendthrift beams from a bright satellite, scaffolding of living light. Iridescent energy: a spume.

The wind plays at the tops of trees, a wintry campaign finally just passing through. But as cold as Old Percy! Love wanes, then returns. *Overly, overly:* a Renaissance

harp-tune. The music of dreams one soon must forget. All quiet on the circle, cars dormant. Follow the moon, follow it back. Wearing a costume, feeling festooned.

Lost deep in the Wenceslaus woods, once up a chimney. Frost outlines my mummy-footprints. The blue beam of my penlight—oh, the fullness when you were there!

Occluded, you pass out of sight. Then again you appear, shapeshifter, pearl of the goat-sky—glow-orbed, double-exposed—while the dustbins stand in their vigil below.

Do Just It

My daughter, because she is nattering on her cell phone,
misses an important plot twist in Bend it Like Beckham.
I thought Jess was going to marry that guy, she says,
finally looking up. No, Tony was just saying that, I reply.
He's actually gay and was just trying to do her a favor;
but she won't let him make the sacrifice. *Uh?* she replies,
confused. I worry that her aesthetic experience of the film
is less pure because she trying to be in two places at once.

My student Justin has his cell phone out the next day during
our class discussion of Zen. I do not appreciate this irony.
I tell him that multi-tasking is the enemy of that philosophy,
that when you eat you should eat, when you sleep just sleep.
There is no growth in concentration where the focus is split.
It is like the koan of Seijo who moves to the city but whose
soul remains in the country. When she dies, where does
she go? One answer: *Nowhere*, because there isn't enough
spiritual energy left concentrated in any one place.

When you only half-pay attention, Justin, the net gain isn't
half, but zero. Motto of a contemplative life: Do Just It.

This Poem

does not come accompanied
with an *Estimated Reading Time*
to help you decide to commit.

is not about my search
for the Other.   The other what?

is not on any particular theme
such as public transport,
prairie dogs, or the chill of space.

is not exclusively reserved
for persons over sixty-five.

is not gay. Or straight, or
in search of a different identity.

does not deliberately eschew
rhyme (most of the time)

is definitely not going to go
to rehab. No, no, no.

is bound for glory. This poem.

Escape Plan

Develop your own escape plan. When others ask to friend you on Facebook, tell them no. Better yet, start a feud. Real Hatfields and McCoys kind of stuff. Then delete your profile. Pursue all the interests you lied about on that page. No ring tones: set your phone on vibrate and wean yourself off it. Better yet, become absent-minded and forget where you put it. Explore different places. Rediscover nature and just try to appreciate it without the benefit of technology. Do not consider giving someone a running total of your day an urgent need. If emergencies happen, accept them as a backdrop to your life because life is sad. When you take pictures, don't review and edit them immediately. Your life is not a movie, and you are not being paid a per diem to watch the dailies. Do not wear company brands on your clothing unless you are being paid a residual. Put down your Guitar Hero and learn to play for real. And no more violent video games. They may not turn you violent, but they will not bring you peace. Read a book.

Meet someone and ask her to leave virtual reality with you. Plan and pull off a daring escape from the Matrix. Have a family and let the realities of changing diapers and paying down a mortgage sink in. Do not take on a bigger payment than you can afford. Do not live in a McMansion unless you harbor a family of fugitives fleeing an oppressive regime who need a place to stay. Only then would you need the extra room. Learn to navigate thrift stores. Fill your house with modest things. If you live in a gated community, make sure you can get out. Make sure others are not being unfairly kept out. Reconsider instant messaging. Put space in between contacts to allow yourself more time to live and report back. Become legendarily hard to reach, a hermit, a yeti. Then others won't pick up the same stream of chatter whenever they do reach you. If you inhabit a cubicle at work or have a job in which you create nothing, take up poetry or painting. Cut your finger and drip over a canvas before letting that spirit in yourself die.

Reasons For Dialing 911

if there aren't enough checkout lanes open at the store
if you didn't get enough mcnuggets with your order
if you bought a cd and only a couple of songs are OK
if someone's been badmouthing you at your workplace
if there are too many previews before the movie begins
if the birds outside your window won't let you sleep in
if you suddenly can't afford to fill your car up with gas
if rush says the liberals are trying to ruin the whole U.S.
if you're worried about the junk floating around in space
if you haven't gotten e-mail in your inbox for two days
if someone you just friended on facebook doesn't care
if you're alone and just need to know someone's out there

The Carsitters

The carsitters
lurk
in mall lots,
waiting
for their
wives.

Grim faces,
wire-rim
glasses,
eyes faced
forward—

middle-aged men
reined back
by their
own shoulder
straps.

Sometimes,
a Sunday paper
or bulletin
is spread
across the
dash.

At others,
just a silent
death grip
on the
wheel.

AC running,
engine humming,
occasionally

revved,
sounding
like thunder.

I do not know
how
human beings
can sit in
such anger
for hours.

I only know
I do
not
want to mess
with them.

Schedule Adjustment

I see my retirement as a time of liberation, picture myself sitting by a lake, lunching at a favorite restaurant, then settling in with a book for the remainder of the day, or until football comes on. Or getting up early, hiking a desert studded with saguaros, then retreating to a cool portico for an iced tea and a siesta in my chair. Yes exactly: those will be the days. Should be a hoot!

Unless, the nearer those golden years approach, the less agile my mind becomes. And I begin to lean in closer to address my students, who start to seem like a second family to me. And peer over my half-glasses, determined to recall first names, and scan the glazed faces to spark any memory I can of my daughter and her friends. Smiling at the young people and shaking my head,

recalling the times as a single father I was forever working or commuting, planning elaborate play-dates and parties on weekends, then letting the kids trash the house. Maybe cadging just a few seconds during an orientation meeting like this one to jot notes on the back of a schedule adjustment form, half-attending to the announcements. But knowing that these days hold ore in them, too.

End Of the Line

for Billy Collins

I'm not looking forward to giving up poetry, to seeking distraction in projects
and household repairs. Going out to cut the grass whether it needs cutting
or not, wearing a floppy hat and an old t-shirt that reads, *He's O.K. Folks!*

I'm not looking forward to giving up poetry, to just studying the calendar
and taking aim at one week or the next. Trying to get the bills and paychecks
to mate while fretting over my 401K, never feeling fully vested in the moment.

I'm not looking forward to giving up poetry, to turning the car stereo up
so I won't have to think and drive. Preferring Sports Talk to the silence
needed to turn an idea around in my head like a roast suckling pig on a spit.

I'm not looking forward to giving up poetry, to packing away my Chagall print,
my surrealist vase, my dream catcher. All the charms I used to coax out of hiding
my subconscious mind, that shy kitten always crouched beneath the ottoman.

I'm not looking forward to giving up poetry, to just skimming the cream off
the surface of life. Seeing my aging self in the mirror with a blank expression
that doesn't change (and not recognizing anything Dorian Gray about this).

I'm not looking forward to giving up poetry, to finding my poems trapped in
an epochal past. Joking, *I don't know where they came from,* those fossils,
remains of an evolutionary branch that proliferated a brief while, then died out.

Immensities

Immensities

One note from a flute:
silent symphony.

Two brush strokes upon the page:
mountain to rival the clouds.

Underscore, forward slash:
boat crossing uncharted seas.

Sown handful of seeds:
the scattered stars.

Blank canvas:
open world of possibilities.

Dark canvas:
universal cover of night.

One frown: sworn enemies for life.
One smile: growing old together.

The Paradine Case

It is a moment of Orpheus ascending
when Louis Jourdan is announced
and enters the courtroom: we see
the slight startled tilt of Valli's head
in the foreground as she struggles
to keep her back turned to him.
Then the camera pulls away,
orbiting left of her as he crosses right,
creating an invisible vector between
two lovers obliged to conceal love.
Just as his steps cross the line,
she can deny herself no longer, turning
her head to steal one backward glance.
In that instant all is known, and lost.

Galago

Graciously, Jasper picks up the tab,
spreading the slip
on the table mat.

Let me just add this, he says, adding
bits of straw (shreddings
from Huck Finn's hat).

Gluing the strands into catenary curves,
the modernist affixes his name
with a flourish.

Too late to redeem the bill
from the waiter! Who remains unaware
of its worth—

in the kitchen passes,
voices are shrill. We sip the remains
of our glasses.

The Director Is an Idiot

I stood among the other actors, waiting to be picked.
I was auditioning for the part of Middle-aged Doctor,
a watery-eyed stoic who had seen it all.

One honey blonde had been picked for Girl at the Bar,
One twenty-year-old for Bartender.
Two girlfriends had to pretend to just meet.
Two guys were placed at a table and told to talk.

The director gave me little more than a glance.
I was too old for the film in his mind, not the right look.
Sensing an opening, the blonde asked about the doctor's part.
The man did not seem surprised. *Interesting*, he said.
This material is kind of dark, kind of noir.

I left to take a bathroom break, entering a makeshift area
without partition between the men's and women's sections.
When I returned, the rehearsal was in full swing.
What do you think? The director asked absently,
obviously having forgotten who I was.

I looked around. The dudes in the booth were chattering.
The set was too bright. Past a crowded line of extras,
the bartender poured drinks to a loud techno beat.
More drink orders were shouted. It felt like a fiesta.

I thought this material was supposed to be dark, I said.
I walked over to the table and told one man to be quiet.
You have just lost your job, I coached. *Say nothing.
This man is your acquaintance, just meeting you for a
drink. He doesn't know you well enough to care.*

The blonde was busy trying to comb out her hair.
I walked over to her, removing a pair of wire–rim glasses
much too wide for her face. Then I returned to the director.
*Tell your new girlfriend to go back to her original mark
and to try not to look so perky!*

I handed the astonished man the spectacles.
Here, I say. *Put these on and stand over there.*
Whoever said that you could direct?

Can we have some quiet in here?

The Humanities In Space

We had just opened up the engines and gained altitude
when we felt a thump outside the shuttle.
I hope this thing isn't designed to run on nuclear power,
I said, considering the ramifications of an explosion.

The others in the conference room assured me it was not.
It runs on cohesion, one offered.
I wonder if a hatch blew open, another speculated.
Sensing that the men's words were idle,

I exited down a metal staircase
to check on the panels myself: no problem there.
I returned to make my report. By this time,
the entire ship was undergoing emergency procedures.

Each crew member had been asked to record
a coded sequence of numbers on the station panels.
All were writing furiously, but awkwardly,
as though unaccustomed to pen and paper.

As the shuttle lost altitude, I finished my copying
and went to look out the viewing screen.
Just ahead in the sky, I spotted the enemy craft,
a makeshift plane, jagged like a bat wing.

The shuttle fired upon it, and perhaps scored a hit—
then abruptly banked and brought the eastern hills into view.
There, I saw a row of a thousand small jeeps and tanks,
swathed heads of chieftains, arms wielding scimitars.

I left to find my colleague, a drama teacher,
to pass along to him the bad news. A procrastinator,
he was still copying down his portion of the code.
We felt our craft start to bump and roll,

then some muffled war whoops and motors outside,

where the grounds of a university appeared.
The shuttle was veering toward a group of men
cross-dressed, who gestured and waved to us.

They were clearly in a celebratory mood,
singing while directing our craft to the left.
Ah, it's the gay men's theatre troupe,
my colleague remarked.

We taxied off in the direction they had pointed,
to a long track running alongside athletic fields.
In the cockpit, the pilots saw their chance to take off.
We were going to make our escape!

Good thing I registered us for a theatre membership,
my colleague commented, as we returned to our seats.
Who? I asked him. *Us. The whole space program.*

I thought of the hordes suddenly thwarted in their attack,
then of the dancing and performing men:
It will not go easily for them, I said.

Don't worry, my colleague reassured me.
The fundamentalists won't go anywhere near them.

My Dream Tucson

Winding hills in the distance. A slow establishing track through dusty streets. A swap meet. A Southside restaurant with lit trees, a midtown fiesta with neat mariachis. An even band of streets on the north side of campus near the university sign. A wash winding between residences, a haven for desert green. The old guest house, now in an advanced state of dilapidation, set off in a vacant lot. Palm trees circling a park near a used bookstore. The street passing by the Arizona Inn. Mountains—one climbed my first week there, all barren at the top except for power lines. Hippo shape in the Rincons projecting above a swimming pool. A natural pool. An old cowboy trail leading through tall saguaros close by the Big A. Parking lots sprawling to the east of campus —forever searching through them for a space to park my scooter. The Modern Languages building noticeably new, now a high-rise with elevators to take to get to the office. My mail piled up there.

The Rollerbladers At 3 AM

It is bright, *pre-ter-naturally* bright for three a.m., and you are riding as a passenger in your own car, and there are two men zigzagging in and out through the traffic, holding bottles and looping around the street in easy arcs, and you wonder if they are collecting for some charity, but they aren't, just looping around your car to speak to you casually through the half-open window, and you listen intently for the whir of their wheels. All these things are being recorded on the very surface of the brain and can have no analogue: you are riding home as a passenger in your own car, being driven home by a friend who is gay and you aren't, and it is a short drive but you have gotten lost from your academic conference, lost back many blocks to the downtown area where you once wished to stop but had no time, and now the street is clear because there are so few cars left at three a.m., which is a kind of beauty, and it is *pre-ter-naturally* bright, and the two men coast in and out through the traffic, and rising over the whole scene you recall the face of a colleague smiling like Maya Angelou, asking you to explain a poem back at the conference. All these things are being recorded on the very surface of the brain, to be seen once then forgotten, for they can have no analogue, and exist only in the moment.

I Dreamed I Had Three Different Houses

I dreamed I had three different houses, one just moved out of and one just moved into, and I was sleeping in the new one with boxes wife and child, but I was too restless to remain on the couch, so I walked down the drive and around the next block, where I saw an in-between bachelor house with two bikes on the grass in front, and my car of three car's past parked in the garage, a white Toyota Corolla. Everything was neat and orderly in front, and fondly I recalled the driveway's smooth ascent from the street, where all was quiet now in the early morning darkness. I fumbled for the old key in my pocket, wondering if anyone lived here now and what I would say to them, but then put my mind at rest with a single, charm-like sentence: *You could stay here, too.*

Soon after, I was in the house trying to write my dream down on a phone message pad, but a child who couldn't sleep walked into the study, so I crossed to the kitchen counter, where I began to scribble around the edges of yesterday's newspaper, until that room began to fill with hungry late-night artists. I needed quiet and entered the next room, anxious because I was losing my train of thought, and pulled the top off an organ bench to use as a writing table; instantly, the organ filled with air and began to wheeze a fugue, and a chorus of nuns filed through the room, murmuring. In a final burst, I tore a sheet from a ledger, not caring what was printed on back, and wrote in an elegant flourish:
I dreamed I had three different houses. Then my brother entered, and I awoke.

American Dream

I only have to go back to my great-grandparent's generation
to find a pioneering Alger hero or two. Immigrants, all:
the orphan from Australia who grew up to be state senator,
the French-Canadian bar owner, the Italian fruit traders
who settled in decent Chicago neighborhoods to become
prosperous shopkeepers, policemen, salesmen, and soldiers.

My grandparents and parents shared the same suburban dream:
the house with the white picket fence, the six to eight kids,
the station wagons that produced carbon signatures the size
of John Hancock's. Then, one job per household was enough,
and there were neighborhood potlucks and strange creatures
known as housewives. These were the original life coaches.

My generation plugged guitars into those garages, dreamed
of selling a screenplay or starting up a band. We watched
a lot of TV, worked part time jobs, went to college, spent
junior years abroad. We were restless, got hired and fired,
married and divorced, learned to manage family and career.
But we never discarded that script, if you'd care to take a look.

They say the new American Dream is winning the lottery,
or gaining instant fame on reality TV, whether one has talent
or not. But that is an old dream, really: prospector's gold,
striking it rich. It may be that all dreams need to cycle out,
and all those who don't get their fifteen minutes of fame this
go-around might have to start over again at the bottom.

My Celebrity Dreams

Spring 2008

I was in Iraq with Dick Cheney on a press junket. We were standing in the middle of a field where a log was a hanging by a thin band to a tree.

Cheney went over and kicked it off, a photo op intended to symbolize that the country was under control. I retrieved the log, took it back to the U.S. in the plane. Then wrapped it and brought it to Al Franken, whose Minnesota campaign office was in rear of a gift shop.

—

I dreamed that my daughter, Ellen Page, couldn't speak to her teacher on first day of school even though she had carefully rehearsed what to say and had been assigned to write a letter of introduction. Frustrated, I pinched her cheeks to get her to talk, then awoke instantly, ashamed. Same dream the next night and the next, this time with Ellen Page morphing into a Chinese exchange student. Next week at the university, I stood up for ESL students who had been getting no support.

—

Tom Brady came by to visit w/family and seemed relieved for break from the limelight. Said he would become free @1:00 after the Super Bowl to join my friends in a game of cards—"Hearts with Sticks and Grains in it."

—

Visited Alfred Hitchcock in a retirement home. He was interested in the film course I taught, wanted a for-instance of how I approached style. I pulled out a penlight and illustrated different lighting techniques. He indulged me in this, though he didn't consider lighting the province of the director—rather, in his mind, only an adjunct technical feature.

—

I was in church: Barak Obama was my pastor.

—

I was a cast member of *Saturday Night Live* and brought my new blonde companion to read her earnest poem on air. It got mixed reviews, and I tried to defend her to the rest of the cast, comparing her to Victoria Jackson and saying it wasn't always necessary to go directly for laughs. Then again, I had to wonder if that was really helping the cause of someone whose poems had not been intentionally ironic, or simply exposing her to further ridicule. After the performance I waited for Victoria in the limo. Either she had gotten lost en route, or pulled away with someone else.

—

Alfred Hitchcock was showing my class a Werner Herzog film while a small alligator ran about under our feet. *Nothing to worry about, just watch the toes. A good way to discourage the wearing of sandals!* Film ended quite unusually for Herzog with removal of the fourth wall and the conquistadors looking straight into the camera: *It's not us, you're the reality. And the breakdown of civilization and decay of law back into nature are images of your world*

—

I was Charles Foster Kane. In my bedroom I had Asian art, including a live woman sitting in silent tableau who represented the spirit of poetry. She had overheard that today was a holiday promoting the arts and had broken her silence, coming down from her position on the wall. I was astounded that she was a living woman, and a beautiful one at that, but waved her onward to do as she wished.

Later, I came across her at an airline desk, desperately trying to catch a flight back to China with no money. I reflected: here was a woman who had been witness to my private life, who had watched over me every night for years as I slept. There followed a melodramatic conversation: *It's not your services I require any longer: I want you to be my wife.* I (or rather Charles, the perspective shifted to 3rd person) began to babble in Chinese and a pact was sealed.

Flash-forward to ten years later, a child in tow. A stop-off in the Kane library where a book binder was procrastinating over the covering of an old volume. Reprimanded, he responded by pretending to be engaged in a highly technical procedure and offering to involve Kane, who was all too easily duped by falsely collegial tactics. Afterwards, Kane tromped back happily to rejoin wife and daughter. Two incongruous dogs in tow, a Russian wolfhound and a Chihuahua.

—

A film somewhat like *Rashomon*, also by a Japanese director, albeit with "superior film grammar," according to my professor, who resembled Richard Dreyfuss, and who excitedly told me he had written an early paper on it as I dashed around the film hall after the screening with him.

The plot concerned the kidnapping and death of a precious pet bird, reputed to be buried on the estate by a nobleman, who callously recounts what he has done. After all, it's only a bird: so he is not punished and walks away contemptuously at the end. What detectives have done, to actually exhume the animal, ends up looking ridiculous. Some ambiguity re. whether we are referring to a bird or a person throughout, so revered was the royal pet.

———

Two similar *Seinfeld*-related dreams. The *Seinfeld* connection served to install me in a large city and instantly define a background group of friends. The first: George gets lost en route to rejoining group. Has to negotiate series of tunnels and slides leading from his apartment to an entertainment venue. Is not fully dressed. In the middle of the city having to locate replacement shirt, pants, gloves, etc. The shirt is found immediately, filched from sample rack. Other articles have to be bartered for or garnered from lost & founds. Arrives wearing a ridiculous hodge-podge of clothing, only just on time.

The second: Elaine has tickets for a play and man is to meet her later. She has playfully written a message on his head, but the chemical has burned into the scalp and caused partial memory loss; the man, who looks like Michael Stipe, can't remember the venue or read the top of his head. He ends up wandering through town, back to a campus dorm where he had once lived, sees his name (Michael) on an old housing list. Bumps into an old girlfriend, who is still somewhat bitter and unaware of his condition. Along with her friends, they go out together.

At a park, digging in a sandbox, the man is becoming more and more of a simpleton, but is happy to have found a group willing to take care of him. Later, the message on his head is noticed when his ex-girlfriend angrily shaves it down to the scalp.

Then a friend there begins to sing a song from an alternative pop group. Michael begins to sing along and is instantly recognized as the singer. *You mean I'm rich?*, he asks. *You mean we could all be rich? Would you like to be rich too?* Carrying on, still not remembering, yet excited that he has finally done something right.

———

A party in So. Cal. at which Wayne Gretzky was a guest. We hung out together.

—

The Incredible Hulk was rampaging through the city, bearing down near my parent's home, his yelling and growling a constant noise in the background. He was as large as a water tower, larger, and each dragged foot was enough to wipe out a city block. I myself was super-sized, and along with another superhero was punching and pushing at a wall of water, lifting and directing the waves at Hulk, trying to bury him. The tide didn't rise quite high enough, but made him sufficiently angry to growl and head our way, so we lured him away from the populated area.

I then abandoned my partner and returned home. The power was out; I stood in front of the bathroom mirror and tried to find my toothbrush in a neat pile near the sink. The growling could still be heard in the distance. I prayed that my partner could continue the deluge. The power clicked back on in the house, and I suddenly saw my young brothers and sisters huddled around the stairs, looking shabby but relieved that the pogrom with its terrifying siren-like drone had passed over our home.

—

On site of a Hollywood scandal: a lake house murder. Actors gathered to reconstruct the characters and events. A naked Madonna, bathing in a tureen of tomato soup.

My Mars Dream

I brush the lavender sand aside with my glove
to find a layer of bright green turf underneath—
only a movie set, after all.

Taps are available for sampling Mars lager.
I fill a cup from a gummed-up stopper and taste.
It is dream-smooth.

An Anomaly has the effect of resetting time
for those trapped in its cloud. I keep stepping in
just to restart a conversation.

A slow-moving land rover grounds to a halt
in the gravel. One astronaut, impatient at the delay,
loosens his grip and floats off.

To net him, an older pilot uses plastic drink rings.
The deranged man is smoking a cigar, murmuring
Welcome to Old Mexico.

I drift backward through a field of constellations,
plucking down satellites and secreting them away
for my young daughter.

About the Author

M[ichael] V[incent] Montgomery is a native of Minneapolis, Minnesota and a graduate of Macalester College in St. Paul. He spent a year on an international study scholarship to Cambridge University and completed his M.A. and Ph.D. at the University of Arizona. He is currently a professor in the General Education Department at Life University in Marietta, Georgia, where he teaches courses in English, film, and philosophy. His poetry has appeared in many journals and e-zines such as *Babel Fruit, Bird's-Eye ReView, Conversation Poetry Quarterly, Dream People, Eudaimonia Poetry Review, Honeyland Review,* qarrtsiluni, RHYTHM, Sleet, Tangent Literary Arts Magazine, and Words-Myth. He lives in the Atlanta area with his daughter.